Ivy Glo

SSAT & ISEE
VOCABULARY 3, EDITION 2.0

MADE WITH CARE
....

NEW YORK

This publication was written and edited by the team at Ivy Global.

Editors: Sacha Azor and Natalia Irizarry-Cole

Producers: Lloyd Min and Junho Suh

Contributors: Alexandra Candib, Lei Huang, WooKyung Lee, Jonathan Li, Gideon Ng, Yolanda Song, Adam Wolsky, and Nicole Young

About Ivy Global

Ivy Global is a pioneering education company that produces high-quality educational material.

E-mail: publishing@ivyglobal.com
Website: http://www.ivyglobal.com

Copyright 2019 © by Ivy Global. All rights reserved.

Introduction

Welcome, students and parents! This pocketbook is intended to help students prepare for the level of vocabulary encountered on the SSAT & ISEE. For students applying to many top private and independent schools in North America, these exams are a crucial and sometimes daunting step in the admissions process. By helping you master these core vocabulary words, Ivy Global will help you build your confidence and maximize your score on these important exams.

Comprehensive Prep

We know that no two students are exactly alike—each student brings unique personal strengths to his or her test preparation. For this reason, we've tailored our preparation materials to help students with a specific subject area or goal. Ivy Global also offers full sets of SSAT and ISEE books to help students develop the best strategies for each section of these exams:

- *SSAT English, SSAT Math, SSAT Practice*
- *ISEE English, ISEE Math, ISEE Practice*

This book is the third in a set of three vocabulary pocketbooks for the SSAT and ISEE that include a total of 365 words for every-day learning:

- *Vocabulary 1* (Essential) – Words 1-125
- *Vocabulary 2* (Extended) – Words 126-250
- *Vocabulary 3* (Advanced) – Words 251-365

Ivy Global's products are available for purchase at ivyglobal.com/products or amazon.com.

How to Use This Book

This book is a study aid; it isn't a complete dictionary. The words here are selected because they are likely to be useful when studying for the SSAT and ISEE, and we've given brief definitions to help you quickly learn the most common meaning of each word. There is more information available about each word, including information about less common definitions and the history and etymology of each word.

- When you learn a word, pay attention to its part of speech (is it a noun, verb, adjective, or adverb?) and look for other possible definitions of the word.
- Be sure to write your own personal sentence for each word to help you remember it.
- When you're writing your sentence, if you don't totally understand the meaning of a word you should try to search for other sentences containing the word.
- Use a pencil, and have a trusted reader check your sentences.
- Correct your sentences if you don't quite capture the meanings of the words on your first try.
- In order to master as many words as possible before your exam, create a daily schedule and make sure to review old words while you are learning new ones.

Sample Study Schedule

To begin, try using this sample study plan as a model for your own personalized study schedule.

Sample Study Schedule		
Week	Words this Week	Goal Reached?
1	1 - 25	☐
2	26 - 50	☐
3	51 - 75	☐
4	76 - 100	☐
5	101 – 125	☐
6	Final Review	☐

We recommend focusing on 10-40 words each week. The table above is for a schedule of learning 25 words per week.

Learning New Words

As you work through these vocabulary words, make sure that you're using the most effective strategies.

Use mnemonics: Mnemonics are devices to help improve your memory and can be used to help you remember difficult words. They can use combinations of words, images, patterns of letters or a myriad of other things. Mnemonic devices should only be used with words that are complex—short, easy to remember words can actually become more complicated with the use of a mnemonic device. Mnemonics help you convert abstract information into a mix of what you already know.

You can use similar sounding words to remember a new one:

- There are no sirens in this serene neighborhood.

Siren is something that is loud and annoying, but serene means "calm and clear." A lack of sirens will make for a serene environment.

- The wrecking ball was raised to raze the building.

Raze means "destroy," and a wrecking ball would probably get the job done.

You can also use something more visual:

- Novel tea would be a novelty. Usually tea is made from plants, not books!

Expand your classroom: Don't think of learning vocabulary as something you need to do just for the SSAT or ISEE. Instead, try to make these words a part of your everyday life. There are lots of creative ways you can use your new vocabulary words:

- Start using the words you learn in essays and homework assignments.
- Try making a tricky word your theme for an art project.
- Use new words in conversations with friends and family.
- Tape flash cards or put sticky notes with the words you're learning around your house and recite the definition of a word each time you see it.
- Compete with your friends to see who can master the most words.
- Draw a picture that captures the meaning of a word.

Know Connotations: A word's connotation is its secondary meaning, or the feeling we get from the word. A word can have a positive (+) connotation if it means something good, a negative (-) connotation if it means something bad, or a neutral connotation if it is neither good nor bad.

For example, the word "horrible" has a negative connotation, whereas "joyous" has a positive connotation. If you can remember that a word means something positive or negative, you may be able to eliminate answer choices with the opposite connotation if you encounter them on your exam.

Come up with contexts: If you want to remember multiple definitions of a word, one useful strategy is to come up with many contexts—phrases where you might have heard the word before. A word's context is everything in a phrase or sentence that might influence the word's meaning. The word "charge," for example can have many different meanings, depending on its context. It might be helpful to make yourself a bubble chart and think of as many phrases as you can:

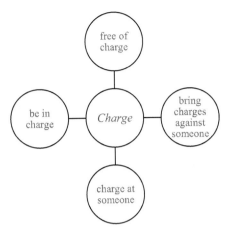

What does "charge" mean in each of these contexts? "Free of charge" means that you don't have to pay for something; to "be in charge" means to have power or be in control; to "charge at someone" means to attack suddenly or assault; and to "bring charges against someone" means to accuse or blame.

Let's begin!

abeyance

Ivy Global

temporary inactivity or suspension (n)

After Josh was caught sneaking out past curfew, his allowance was held in abeyance until his parents felt he had once again earned their trust.

Your sentence:

abnegate

Ivy Global

renounce, reject (v)

The students felt that by not adequately preparing them for college-level work, their English teacher had abnegated her responsibility as an educator.

Your sentence:

abstain

Ivy Global

avoid, refrain from (v)

In the weeks leading up to the exam, he abstained from going out with friends on weeknights so that he could focus on studying.

Your sentence:

_____
_____
_____
_____
_____
_____

abyss

Ivy Global

a deep pit; something that seems endlessly deep (n)

She had recurring nightmares about falling endlessly into a dark abyss.

Your sentence:

acrimonious

Ivy Global

angry, bitter (adj)

Despite the moderator's pleas for civility, the debate quickly turned acrimonious as arguments devolved into personal attacks.

Your sentence:

_____

_____

_____

_____

_____

_____

acumen

Ivy Global

sharp insight; good judgment (n)

She was never a stellar student, but her business acumen carried her far in her career as an entrepreneur.

Your sentence:

admonish

scold, reprimand; advise (v)

When he returned after his illness, Mr. Perez admonished his students for being so disrespectful to their substitute teacher.

Your sentence:

amalgamate

Ivy Global

combine into one (v)

After the two companies amalgamated, the newly formed organization controlled more than half the market in its industry.

Your sentence:

anachronistic

in the wrong time period; outdated (adj)

The movie's elaborate 17th-century costumes looked impressive to audiences, but they were actually highly anachronistic considering that the story took place in 1834.

Your sentence:

_____

_____

_____

_____

_____

_____

analogous

similar or comparable in a specific way (adj)

Giving someone else the password to your email is analogous to giving him or her a copy of your mailbox key.

Your sentence:

_____

_____

_____

_____

_____

_____

antecede

Ivy Global

come before (v)

Murasaki Shikibu's *The Tale of Genji*, often considered the world's first novel, antecedes the development of English-language novels by at least five hundred years.

Your sentence:

antiquated

Ivy Global

old-fashioned, outdated (adj)

Many teachers are starting to consider pure lecture classes to be an antiquated mode of education that does not prepare students for the challenges of the modern world.

Your sentence:

_____
_____
_____
_____
_____
_____

apex

Ivy Global

the highest point (n)

From the apex of the mountain, you can't see anything above you but bright blue sky.

Your sentence:

apparatus

Ivy Global

an instrument or system designed or organized for a specific purpose (n)

Their first chemistry class was spent learning about the different pieces of the laboratory apparatus they would use for their experiments.

Your sentence:

_____
_____
_____
_____
_____
_____

artifact

Ivy Global

an object made by a human being (n)

Archaeologists study ancient artifacts to gain insight into the cultures of the associated time period.

Your sentence:

attenuate

make smaller; weaken (v)

There's no cure for the common cold, but some medications can attenuate its symptoms.

Your sentence:

baleful

Ivy Global

threatening; hostile (adj)

He had the ability to ward off potential bullies with a single baleful look.

Your sentence:

bedlam

Ivy Global

uproar and confusion (n)

The field trip to the zoo descended into total bedlam when some peacocks wandered by the lunch area, scaring the children.

Your sentence:

behemoth

Ivy Global

something enormous or monstrous (n)

It's hard to believe that scientists consider tiny birds to be the last living relatives of the dinosaurs, the behemoths that walked the planet millions of years ago.

Your sentence:

_____
_____
_____
_____
_____
_____

belittle

Ivy Global

make someone or something seem or feel unimportant (v)

In order to show her coworkers that they couldn't get away with belittling her contributions to the team, she filed an official complaint.

Your sentence:

bellicose

warlike; eager to fight (adj)

The bellicose firefighters got into a brawl with another group while the building they had all come to save burned to the ground.

Your sentence:

callow

inexperienced, immature (adj)

The young writer was talented but callow; his stories were entertaining but lacked the maturity that comes from lived experience.

Your sentence:

cataclysm

Ivy Global

a violent event (n)

During a presidential campaign, it's common for supporters of both sides to suggest that electing the opposing candidate will be a cataclysm for our society.

Your sentence:

clandestine

Ivy Global

done in secret (adj)

The secret agent went undercover to infiltrate the mob's clandestine meetings.

Your sentence:

_____

_____

_____

_____

_____

_____

coax

persuade gently (v)

He managed to coax the professor into giving him an extension by emphasizing how thrilled he was to be taking her class.

Your sentence:

_____

_____

_____

_____

_____

_____

compunction

Ivy Global

a sense of guilt after doing something wrong (n)

What really angered the public was that the CEO showed no compunction for stealing millions of dollars.

Your sentence:

_____
_____
_____
_____
_____
_____

confluence

Ivy Global

an act of merging (n)

When she got promoted and engaged on the same day, it felt like a confluence of all her biggest dreams.

Your sentence:

_____

_____

_____

_____

_____

_____

congenial

pleasant; well-suited to one's tastes (adj)

After feeling out of place at several of his roommate's loud parties, he found the members of the book club to be quite congenial company.

Your sentence:

_____
_____
_____
_____
_____
_____

congenital

present from birth (adj)

It was fortunate that the doctors caught her congenital heart defect when she was still a baby, so that they could monitor the problem and quickly discover if it became severe.

Your sentence:

contaminate

make impure or dirty (v)

Acid rain means that chemicals can contaminate water supplies far from the original sources of pollution.

Your sentence:

criterion

Ivy Global

a standard used in evaluation (n)

For most employers, punctuality is as important a criterion as an impressive résumé, so make sure you show up to job interviews on time.

Your sentence:

_____
_____
_____
_____
_____
_____

denude

make bare (v)

The burglars denuded his home of everything but the furniture.

Your sentence:

destitute

Ivy Global

lacking the necessities of life (adj)

During the Great Depression, many once affluent families became destitute because they could not find jobs.

Your sentence:

din

Ivy Global

a loud, prolonged, and unpleasant noise (n)

Having lived next to a construction site for several months, I remember having to listen to the awful din of jackhammers and bulldozers.

Your sentence:

elucidate

Ivy Global

make clear, explain (v)

She struggled with English class until she had a teacher who could elucidate the paper-writing process in a way that made her finally understand what she had been missing.

Your sentence:

_____
_____
_____
_____
_____
_____

enjoin

instruct or urge; command (v)

Peter Stuyvesant enjoined residents of New Amsterdam to clean their chimneys and take care of their garbage.

Your sentence:

ennui

Ivy Global

weariness from having nothing to do; boredom (n)

The worst part of being home sick was the ennui that set in when she felt well enough to want to do something, but still too sick to go anywhere.

Your sentence:
_____
_____
_____
_____
_____
_____

ersatz

Ivy Global

artificial; used as a substitute (adj)

Ersatz diamonds might not be as beautiful as the real thing, but they're much more affordable.

Your sentence:

_____
_____
_____
_____
_____
_____

eruption

Ivy Global

a sudden outbreak or explosion (n)

The eruption of zits on her cheeks felt looked like she had been out in the sun and was now flushed and red.

Your sentence:

_____
_____
_____
_____
_____
_____

exasperate

irritate intensely (v)

His children's whining exasperated him, but he understood that long car rides were hard for toddlers, so he strove to stay positive when he talked to them.

Your sentence:
_____
_____
_____
_____
_____
_____

facsimile

Ivy Global

an exact copy (n)

The museum displayed a facsimile of the rare 12th century manuscript to ensure that the real document would stay safe from crowds.

Your sentence:

_____

_____

_____

_____

_____

_____

feasible

Ivy Global

very possible (adj)

Although it would have been nice to build a two-story set for the musical, it simply wasn't feasible to do so in the four weeks they had.

Your sentence:

fidelity

Ivy Global

faithfulness, loyalty (n)

Her fidelity to her ideals in the face of cynicism was truly inspiring.

Your sentence:

_____

_____

_____

_____

_____

_____

filch

steal casually (v)

On his last day at the job, he filched some supplies from the office cabinet.

Your sentence:

fraught

Ivy Global

tense; filled with or likely to result in something negative (adj)

The thieves' plan was fraught with risk, yet somehow they eluded capture.

Your sentence:

_____
_____
_____
_____
_____
_____

fret

Ivy Global

visibly worry (v)

She constantly fretted over her college applications, which made for many sleepless nights.

Your sentence:

_____

_____

_____

_____

_____

_____

fulsome

Ivy Global

excessive; overly flattering (adj)

He thought he was being suave, but his fulsome praise just made her embarrassed.

Your sentence:

galvanize

Ivy Global

shock or excite into taking action (v)

Mary Harris "Mother" Jones's moving and powerful speeches galvanized workers around the country into banding together to fight for their rights.

Your sentence:

_____

_____

_____

_____

_____

_____

garrulous

excessively talkative (adj)

His garrulous nature could make him an exhausting person to talk to, but at least there was never an awkward silence.

Your sentence:

_____

_____

_____

_____

_____

_____

genesis

Ivy Global

origin (n)

Darwin's *On the Origin of Species* formed the genesis of modern evolutionary science.

Your sentence:

gyrate

Ivy Global

move in a circle or spiral (v)

As part of their program, figure skaters must gyrate incredibly quickly on the ice while holding their bodies in special positions.

Your sentence:

harbinger

Ivy Global

something that signals the approach of something else (n)

It might feel like summer still, but the flush of red creeping into leaves is a harbinger of autumn's approach.

Your sentence:

hinder

make difficulties for which result in delay (v)

She had been hoping to finish her essay in a few days, but her progress was hindered by a family emergency that took up much of her time.

Your sentence:

_____

_____

_____

_____

_____

_____

homage

Ivy Global

a public honor (n)

On the third Monday in January, the United States pays homage to the legacy of Martin Luther King, Jr.

Your sentence:

_____

_____

_____

_____

_____

_____

hyperbole

Ivy Global

large exaggeration for effect (n)

When I said this was the worst day of my life, I was clearly using hyperbole; in reality, much worse things have happened to me than a pop quiz.

Your sentence:

_____
_____
_____
_____
_____
_____

hypocrite

Ivy Global

a person who acts contrary to his or her stated beliefs (n)

When a district attorney who had vowed to fight corruption was shown to have accepted bribes from mobsters to ignore their crimes, voters were quick to call him a hypocrite.

Your sentence:

ignominy

Ivy Global

public shame (n)

She blushed at the ignominy of having been caught sleeping in class.

Your sentence:

implicate

show someone to be involved in something negative (v)

Once the police presented the evidence against him, he quickly implicated his partner in crime.

Your sentence:

jeremiad

Ivy Global

a drawn out complaint or lamentation (n)

After months of thinking the team was slacking at practice, the coach lashed out at the players with a jeremiad about how they lacked the heart and ambition necessary to become a great team.

Your sentence:

jocund

cheerful (adj)

The teacher's jocund demeanor gave the moody teenagers a boost in their chemistry class.

Your sentence:

_____

_____

_____

_____

_____

_____

kinetic

Ivy Global

related to motion (adj)

Patricia preferred kinetic activities like running and hiking, while her brothers preferred to sit and play video games all day.

Your sentence:

kismet

Ivy Global

fate, destiny (n)

When Juana discovered that she was sitting next to a long-lost friend on the later flight, she realized it was kismet that she had missed her original flight to Chicago.

Your sentence:

_____
_____
_____
_____
_____
_____

lachrymose

sad, tearful (adj)

He almost never cried, but sad movies always made him lachrymose.

Your sentence:

lax

Ivy Global

not strict; relaxed (adj)

The teacher's lax attitude has led to frequent student absences, late arrivals, and instances of students not completing their homework.

Your sentence:

_____

_____

_____

_____

_____

_____

licit

Ivy Global

legal (adj)

The police officer was convinced that the kids were doing something illegal, but skateboarding in the park at 8 pm was a completely licit activity.

Your sentence:

_____
_____
_____
_____
_____
_____

lugubrious

gloomy; looking or sounding sad (adj)

After she lost her dog, Malala was lugubrious and inconsolable, but luckily the dog returned to her home a few days later.

Your sentence:

malaise

Ivy Global

discomfort, uneasiness (n)

For the past several days, Shinji had been bothered by a sense of malaise, even though nothing unusually bad had happened.

Your sentence:

malapropism

unintentional misuse of a word in place of a similar-sounding word (n)

Jessica blurted out a serious malapropism when she introduced herself to the president: "It's an honor to beat you!"

Your sentence:

malfeasance

Ivy Global

illegal activity (n)

When the president was found to be guilty of malfeasance, confidence in the federal government declined rapidly.

Your sentence:

_____

_____

_____

_____

_____

_____

mangle

Ivy Global

disfigure, mutilate (v)

Although the antelope was severely mangled by the lion's attack, it miraculously escaped with its life.

Your sentence:

_____

_____

_____

_____

_____

_____

maxim

Ivy Global

a principle or rule of conduct (n)

When I felt sick after eating too much chocolate, my father repeated the maxim, "Everything in moderation."

Your sentence:

_____
_____
_____
_____
_____
_____

neophyte

Ivy Global

beginner (n)

The dance studio offered classes for people with all levels of experience, from total neophytes to seasoned experts.

Your sentence:

_____

_____

_____

_____

_____

_____

nexus

Ivy Global

connection; link (n)

In the nineteenth century, the docks of New York City were a crucial nexus between European money and American goods.

Your sentence:

nonchalant

Ivy Global

unconcerned; appearing calm (adj)

Timmy tried to act nonchalant and lighthearted at school after Stacy broke up with him, but inside he was utterly heartbroken.

Your sentence:

_____
_____
_____
_____
_____
_____

noncommittal

Ivy Global

not giving clear indication of feeling; evasive (adj)

Politicians are prone to giving noncommittal answers in interviews so that their statements cannot be used against them.

Your sentence:

_____

_____

_____

_____

_____

_____

nostalgia

Ivy Global

longing for the past (n)

Sofía hadn't thought about Argentina for years, but when she saw a poster of Patagonia in a travel agency, she felt a strong sense of nostalgia for her homeland.

Your sentence:

_____
_____
_____
_____
_____
_____

obliterate

Ivy Global

destroy completely (v)

Modern medicine has allowed us to nearly obliterate diseases, such as smallpox, that used to claim many lives.

Your sentence:

_____

_____

_____

_____

_____

_____

obstreperous

noisy and hard to control (adj)

The obstreperous kindergarteners might have overwhelmed someone else, but she was an experienced teacher and knew how to get them to sit still and stop making noise.

Your sentence:

_____

_____

_____

_____

_____

paean

Ivy Global

song or hymn of triumph and praise (n)

After Jim scored the winning goal for his hockey team, the crowd sang a paean in his honor.

Your sentence:

pariah

Ivy Global

outcast (n)

She was a pariah in high school, but college allowed her to find a group of friends.

Your sentence:

paroxysm

Ivy Global

sudden, violent outburst (n)

When Paul was very young, he was prone to paroxysms of rage in class, which were very disturbing for his teachers.

Your sentence:

_____

_____

_____

_____

_____

_____

pathos

Ivy Global

a quality that causes people to feel sympathy and sadness (n)

The film director mostly made comedies, but often infused them with a certain pathos, which gave them a comic and tragic feel at the same time.

Your sentence:

_____

_____

_____

_____

_____

_____

pedigree

Ivy Global

lineage, ancestry (n)

Although Priscilla is rich now, she did not come from a high pedigree, as her grandparents were poor farmers.

Your sentence:

pester

Ivy Global

annoy (v)

I hate it when my younger siblings pester me to play with them while I'm trying to relax after school.

Your sentence:

_____

_____

_____

_____

_____

_____

polyglot

Ivy Global

speaking several languages (adj); a person who speaks several languages (n)

Lorena became a polyglot as a result of growing up in Italy with a mother who spoke Spanish and a father who spoke French.

Your sentence:

ponder

Ivy Global

think carefully about (v)

Before withdrawing from college to become a professional golfer, Nathan had to ponder the consequences of not graduating.

Your sentence:

prolific

Ivy Global

productive, plentiful; fruitful (adj)

J.K. Rowling was a prolific writer in the 1990s and 2000s, completing seven Harry Potter novels in only ten years.

Your sentence:

_____
_____
_____
_____
_____
_____

prolix

Ivy Global

drawn out, wordy (adj)

The *New York Times* piece made some good points, but its prolix character made it hard for readers to stay engaged.

Your sentence:

_____
_____
_____
_____
_____
_____

purloin

take, steal (v)

While George was waiting for the bus, a pickpocket managed to purloin his wallet so stealthily that he didn't notice until he got home.

Your sentence:

_____
_____
_____
_____
_____
_____

quandary

Ivy Global

dilemma; state of uncertainty (n)

When Olivia found twenty dollars on the ground, she was in a quandary about whether she should keep the money or try to find its rightful owner.

Your sentence:

_____
_____
_____
_____
_____
_____

quarrel

dispute, disagreement (n)

Although they had the occasional quarrel, Luis and Chimamanda had a marriage that was relatively conflict-free.

Your sentence:

_____

_____

_____

_____

_____

_____

quotidian

Ivy Global

daily, ordinary (adj)

Mark decided to quit his job at the law firm and start teaching swimming lessons after growing tired of the quotidian and mundane office tasks.

Your sentence:

_____
_____
_____
_____
_____
_____

ravenous

Ivy Global

incredibly hungry (adj)

After sitting on a plane for six hours, Irina was so ravenous that she ate two cheeseburgers at the airport restaurant when she landed.

Your sentence:

_____
_____
_____
_____
_____
_____

recalcitrant

Ivy Global

defying authority (adj)

The teacher worried about Priya's future; although she was bright, she was so recalcitrant that she got sent to detention almost every day.

Your sentence:

relinquish

give up (v)

It was difficult for Zeke to relinquish his favorite stuffed animal, but his parents decided that he was too old to be sleeping with toys.

Your sentence:

_____

_____

_____

_____

_____

robust

Ivy Global

strong, vigorous (adj)

Titanium alloys are used in building spacecraft and airplanes because they are very robust and relatively light.

Your sentence:

sanguine

Ivy Global

optimistic (adj)

Emily's sanguine approach towards teaching inspired her students, and they went into their standardized tests with a positive attitude.

Your sentence:

_____

_____

_____

_____

_____

_____

simulate

Ivy Global

imitate, mimic (v)

To prepare astronauts for leaving Earth, NASA has developed exercises that simulate the conditions of going into space.

Your sentence:

specter

Ivy Global

ghost, spirit (n)

Esteban did not believe the mansion to be haunted until he saw the specter of the previous owner with his own eyes.

Your sentence:

_____

_____

_____

_____

_____

_____

spurn

reject, scorn (adj)

Despite being spurned by taller players when he was younger due to his short stature, Mugsy Bogues became a top-quality professional basketball player.

Your sentence:

_____

_____

_____

_____

_____

stentorian

loud (adj)

Erica's stentorian voice made her an excellent actress for the stage, since she could be heard even in the back of large theaters.

Your sentence:

subterfuge

Ivy Global

deception used to get or hide something (n)

The dictator often used subterfuge to trick people into confessing to crimes they never committed.

Your sentence:

_____

_____

_____

_____

_____

_____

succinct

Ivy Global

informative but brief; concise (adj)

One thing that made Leticia a good manager was her succinct emails, which conveyed necessary information without wasting other people's time.

Your sentence:

_____

_____

_____

_____

_____

synchronous

Ivy Global

occurring simultaneously (adj)

The year 1848 was important for the synchronous political revolutions happening throughout Europe.

Your sentence:

_____

_____

_____

_____

_____

_____

synthesis

Ivy Global

combination of parts to make a whole (n)

A good textbook is a synthesis of the work of hundreds of scholars in the field.

Your sentence:

_____

_____

_____

_____

_____

tarnish

ruin, stain (v)

Yuri tarnished his reputation as a great public speaker when he forgot all of the lines to his speech at the convention.

Your sentence:

terminate

Ivy Global

end, stop (v)

After a very exciting match between two strong teams, the soccer match terminated with no score.

Your sentence:

_____

_____

_____

_____

_____

_____

tome

Ivy Global

thick book (n)

The great Russian writer Leo Tolstoy is well-known for his tomes *War and Peace* and *Anna Karenina*, each spanning over five hundred pages.

Your sentence:

truculent

Ivy Global

eager to fight, aggressive (adj)

Despite the truculent behavior of the apartheid leaders, Nelson Mandela remained peaceful and forgave them when he became the first president of post-apartheid South Africa.

Your sentence:

undermine

threaten, weaken (v)

Darlene constantly undermined the authority of her parents by inviting friends over when they weren't home, even though it was against the rules.

Your sentence:

upbraid

Ivy Global

criticize or scold; find fault with (v)

The students hated the vice principal because he would upbraid them for the slightest uniform infractions.

Your sentence:

_____

_____

_____

_____

_____

_____

verisimilitude

Ivy Global

the appearance of being true or real (n)

The ancient Greek artist Zeuxis supposedly once painted a picture of grapes with such verisimilitude that birds tried to eat them.

Your sentence:

voluble

Ivy Global

talkative; fluent (adj)

Otto's voluble demeanor made him a natural politician, and he quickly rose up the ranks in his party after only a couple of years.

Your sentence:

_____
_____
_____
_____
_____

zenith

Ivy Global

the highest point (n)

The zenith of Karen's career had already passed—no longer was she being sought out by the top design firms.

Your sentence:

_____

_____

_____

_____

_____

_____

zephyr

Ivy Global

gentle wind (n)

Naomi loved living in Santa Monica because she could walk on the pier and feel the zephyr caress her face.

Your sentence:

_____

_____

_____

_____

_____

_____

Made in the
USA
Lexington, KY